THE
SONG of
SONGS

Love Lyrics from the Bible

THE
SONG of
SONGS

A New Translation

MARCIA FALK

Illustrated by Barry Moser

HarperSanFrancisco
A Division of HarperCollins *Publishers*

FIRST HARPERCOLLINS PAPERBACK EDITION PUBLISHED IN 1993

Design by David Bullen

Library of Congress Cataloging-in-Publication Data
Bible. O.T. Song of Solomon. English. Falk. 1993.
    The Song of songs : a new translation / Marcia Falk. —
1st HarperCollins pbk. ed.
        p.   cm.
    ISBN 0-06-250306-5 (alk. paper)
    I. Falk, Marcia.   II. Title.
BS1487.F34   1993
223'.905209 — dc20
                                                    92-53253
                                                    CIP

93 94 95 96 97 MAL 10 9 8 7 6 5 4 3 2

This edition is printed on acid-free paper that meets the
American National Standards Institute Z39.48 Standard.

For Abraham Gilead —
my future and my joy

Contents

THE SONG OF SONGS
Thirty-One Lyric Poems
in Hebrew and in English Translation

Translator's Note:
History and Acknowledgments

The journey of translation always begins with the text. Yet sometimes there is an earlier journey — the story of how the translator came to the text. This book had its origin in the early 1970s, when I was a doctoral student in English and comparative literature at Stanford University and found myself dissatisfied with the limits of the traditional academic curriculum. My growing need, at that time, for sources more directly connected to my own history — as a woman and as a Jew — led me in search of Hebrew literature that included the authentic voices of women. Although I had studied Hebrew Bible from childhood on, I wasn't sure it had what I was now looking for. But then a memory arose of a part of the Bible that had engaged me the first time I heard it chanted, in adolescence. I didn't know much about this particular book; yet, especially as a poet, I felt somehow called to it — if for no other reason than its haunting musicality. As I began to study, I soon saw what a remarkable book this was — one in which the voices of women and men were heard celebrating eros, sensuality, and the pleasures of nature. I was first enchanted, then soon engrossed, in this small, unique Hebrew text — the Song of Songs.

Coincidentally, at the time when I began my study of the Song, I was enrolled in a poets' workshop on verse translation. As I talked with members of the class about my new discovery, I saw that they were unfamiliar with the poetry I was speaking of. Indeed, the Song of Songs that they knew from the standard English versions of the Bible was quite different from the Hebrew text that had me in its thrall. So when my classmates suggested that I try my hand at my own translation, I sat down and began. That beginning eventually led to my doctoral thesis, a translation and study of the Song — which, in turn, led to books, including the gift edition that you now hold in your hands.

When I first began my research for the project, literary analysis of the Bible was relatively untilled terrain; I had to combine the resources of two university departments, English and Religious Studies, in order to evolve my approach to interpretation and translation. Indeed much has changed in the study of literature and of the Bible since that time in the early seventies, when my modest proposal of a literary critique of the Bible that included feminist insights was received by some as shocking. (I recall one professor who cautioned me, early on, to separate myself as a feminist from myself as a translator. I replied that I was grateful not to have to do any such violence to myself, since the Song of Songs was not the sexist text that he apparently took it to be.) I am gratified to find today that my instincts of more than two decades ago, in regard to the selection and interpretation of this book, led me in directions that still feel right, and it is a relief to see that paths I once embarked on more or less alone are now more commonly and comfortably traveled.

And yet, even during that early period, there were a number of people, including Bible scholars, literary critics, and poets, who supported my efforts. To all of them I remain grateful. In particular, I want to reiterate my appreciation to: Edwin Good, of the Stanford Religious Studies Department, who was the first Bible scholar with whom I studied the Song of Songs; Nogah Hareuveni and his staff at Neot Kedumim (the Gardens of Israel) for their help in identifying flora and fauna in the Bible; Chaim Rabin, of the Hebrew Language Department at the Hebrew University, for answering my queries about obscure words in the original text; and Moshe Greenberg, of the Bible Department at the Hebrew University, for debating with me my interpretations of the Hebrew and for encouraging me to persevere at my renditions.

I also wish to acknowledge the Stanford English Department, which provided support and fellowship assistance for several years; the Fulbright-Hays Foundation, which gave me a grant in Bible and Hebrew literature; and the Hebrew

University of Jerusalem, which awarded me a postdoctoral fellowship in Hebrew language and literature to continue my research.

I have been sustained in a different way by the support of several communities — especially the Jewish renewal and *havurah* movements — which have kept my version of the Song of Songs alive for years, beginning before it was ever published and including long periods when it was hard to get or out of print. I was encouraged by hearing my translation read dramatically on radio and stage, set to music and sung, recited at wedding ceremonies, and chanted on the Sabbath of Passover. To all those who embraced my work and made it part of a new oral tradition, I am enormously grateful: you nourished the poet's soul, perhaps more than you know.

Warmest appreciation goes, above all, to Steve Rood, my best and most faithful reader, for his keen and sensitive review of draft upon draft of the latest editions of this work. And to my first teachers — Abraham Abbey Falk, of blessed memory, and Frieda Goldberg Falk — goes my immeasurable gratitude for pointing the way.

Preface

One of the most celebrated collections of ancient love poetry, the Song of Songs — also known in English as the Song of Solomon, and referred to, by scholars, simply as the Song — is the only book of love poetry in the Bible and as such has been the subject of much speculation and controversy. For centuries, both Jewish and Christian traditions viewed the Song as spiritual allegory, thus justifying its place in the biblical canon; but this mode of interpretation, moving and imaginative as it may be, does not explain the text's primary level of meaning. Another centuries-old interpretation presents the Song as a drama with fixed characters, such as King Solomon and a country bride or King Solomon and two country lovers. But it is difficult to find evidence of dramatic structure in the Song; acts, scenarios, and characters are not indicated, and there is hardly a trace of coherent plot. Rather, the Song has a variety of contexts that shift frequently in no apparent dramatic sequence and within which many different kinds of voices speak. There is no reason to assume only a few fixed speakers in the Song, and even less justification for viewing Solomon as a central character. Although Solomon's name is mentioned in the Hebrew title, this title was bestowed not by the Song's original author or authors but by later compilers, who were likely also responsible for giving the text its semblance of structural unity. In its earliest stages, the Song was probably not a unified work at all, but several lyric poems, each having its own integrity.

About the Song's authorship and origins very little is known. Tradition ascribes the work to King Solomon, but this view is discounted by modern scholars, who generally agree that the Song's authorship cannot be specified. Indeed, there is no consensus even about the date of composition, with proposals ranging from 950 to 200 B.C.E.; some hold that the Song was composed by several authors over an extended period of time and compiled between 500 and 200 B.C.E.

In the past two centuries, scholars have hypothesized about the original context and function of the Song, proposing, for example, that it was a cycle of wedding songs or the liturgy of an ancient fertility cult. These theories, however, are not only unprovable but unconvincing, because they attempt to force the varied material in the text into single, confining molds. It is finally simpler and more illuminating to view the Song as a variegated collection of different types of lyric love poems spoken by a variety of speakers—poems that did not all necessarily derive from a single author or serve the same function in their original society. The stylistic similarities and repetitions among the poems are best explained as literary conventions of ancient Hebrew verse, particularly if one accepts the view that the Song was, in its earliest stages, popular oral literature.

Indeed, the Song exhibits all the properties of oral verse. Songlike not just in title but in nature, it has been part of a postbiblical oral tradition for centuries. In Jewish communities, it is still ritually chanted (on the Sabbath of Passover or, among Yemenites, on the eve of every Sabbath), and in Western culture in general, it has been sung and set to music more often and more variously than any other ancient text. I believe it likely that the Song was originally orally composed and transmitted over an extended period before being transcribed, compiled, and finally canonized.

The stylistic and thematic features that characterize the collection as a whole give us at least a partial picture of the culture out of which this poetry emerged—a culture that may not exactly conform to our assumptions or expectations. For example, females speak over half the lines in the Song—an exceptionally large proportion for a biblical text—and, even more remarkably, they speak out of their own experiences and imaginations, in words that do not seem filtered through the lens of patriarchal consciousness (good reasons to presume that women contributed significantly to the oral composition of the Song). In the Song, women and men alike share a range of emotionally expressive action and language: women initiate lovemaking at least as often as men; both female and male voices are at times urgent and assertive, at other times vulnerable and tender. Even the metaphors used to describe the lovers' bodies shatter our stereotypes: both female and male speakers remark upon their beloveds' dovelike eyes, and at one moment in the text a *man* is described as having cheeks like spices, lips like lilies. Taken as a whole, the poems of the Song express strikingly nonsexist attitudes toward heterosexual love, and the reciprocity of feeling between women and men is surely part of the Song's enduring power.

Consonant with this mutuality between the sexes, in the Song no domination exists between human beings and the rest of nature; rather, interrelationship prevails. Depictions of nature — as metaphor, context, and motif — abound, and nature appears in the richness of its myriad manifestations. Neither idealized nor demonized, but portrayed with both intimacy and respect, the world of nature becomes foreground and background to all human activity. That world is vividly portrayed with sensory images — the fragrance of incense and spices, the taste of nectars and fruits, the sounds of birdsongs and human voices, the tender touch of skin. And everywhere sights for the eyes.

As rich as it is in its immediate appeal to the senses, the Song is all the more remarkable for its emotional complexity and depth. Various and sometimes conflicting emotions interlace in the poems; anxiety, loss, frustration, and even hostility are interwoven with erotic and sensual joys. Not all the poems are celebrations, nor are all the poetic contexts idyllic. In urban environments, for example, love relationships are threatened; implied is a tension between public and private domains.

Underlying many poems is the suggestion of a secret love affair, in which the lovers' world must be protected from the critical public eye. Thus the female speaker chases her beloved away by day — not in order to reject him but to postpone their meeting until nighttime, when they can be safely out of view. Sometimes nature itself — which can provide beguiling settings for lovers' rendezvous — becomes an ominous backdrop, serving to keep the lovers apart. Separation of the lovers is a recurrent theme, and lovemaking is more invited, anticipated, imagined, and wished for than actually consummated and fulfilled. Fittingly, even the last poem in the collection ends on a note of separation coupled with the unspoken promise of reunion — a silent anticipation of the moment to come.

Read on the simplest level — without delving into allegory or elaborate hypotheses of structural and contextual unity — the Song reveals itself as a richly textured tapestry, woven from variegated strands of nuance and meaning. The simple level, in other words, need not be superficial; the Song is classic evidence that popular love poetry need not be slight. While it can be enjoyed solely for its surface of sensuous imagery, the Song offers even more to those who will give it a second glance, one that will more deeply pierce its skin.

———

But why this new translation of the Song, a book that has been translated, interpreted, arranged, and — to use Franz Rosenzweig's image — "convulsed" many times? By far the most acclaimed English translation is that found in the King James Version of the Bible, which, although it treats the Song no differently from biblical prose, achieves a level of grace and eloquence that earns it a unique place among English classics. Still, from the perspective of scholarship, the King James Version is long outdated. Our understanding of the Hebrew text has changed considerably since the time of King James, and one of the offshoots of modern research has been a series of new Bible translations. Some of the many new English Bibles that have been completed in the last few decades are *The Revised Standard Version* (1952), *The Jerusalem Bible* (1966), *The New American Bible* (1970), *The New English Bible* (1970), *The New American Standard Bible* (1971), *The Good News Bible: Today's English Version* (1976), *The New International Version* (1978), *The New King James Version* (1982), *The New Jerusalem Bible* (1985), *Tanakh: The Holy Scriptures* (new Jewish Publication Society translation, 1985), *The Revised English Bible* (1989), and *The New Revised Standard Version* (1989). In addition, numerous scholars have produced translations of the Song of Songs, independent of the rest of the Bible. While most of these versions make gestures to indicate that the original is verse, primarily by breaking the text into sections and lines, they tend to lack what poets call simply "language" — the poetic texture and density that mark a text as genuine poetry. Hence the need to go one step further, to combine scholarship with conscious poetic craft and sensibility. This translation is an attempt to fill that need.

The first step in producing this new translation was to reconstruct the Hebrew text as a lyric anthology, offering a visual presentation of it as it might have looked had it been transcribed and preserved the way it was originally recited or sung. The reconstruction presented in this volume — that is, the division of the Song into thirty-one poems and the division of those poems into stanzas and lines — is my own, the result of literary analysis. Although many scholars today view the Song as a collection, the particular decisions concerning where each poem ends and the next begins are not obvious, and no two analyses are exactly alike. This is because the Masoretic text (the standardized Hebrew text, edited by early medieval scholars known as Masoretes), as we have it in the Leningrad manuscript (one of the oldest complete manuscripts of the Hebrew Bible, heavily relied on in contemporary scholarship), presents the Song as an unbroken mass, divided only into roughly equal portions designed for synagogue reading. These divisions, inserted centuries after the time of composition, can hardly be regarded as definitive delineations of the original, orally transmitted poems; every reconstruction is therefore a *postulation* of the original poetic boundaries. Using the text of the Leningrad manuscript, with no alteration of sequence, I divided the Song into poems as I perceived them, basing my decisions on such considerations as changes in speaker, audience, setting, tone of voice, mood, and argument.

The next step was to translate the Hebrew poems individually, giving each its own form in English. I composed the English poems in stanzas and lines according to the felt demands of English poetic craft; these prosodic divisions do not necessarily correspond to those in the Hebrew. I translated the entire Song of Songs with the exception of chapter 6, verse 12 — a line that has plagued commentators for centuries and for which I could arrive at no satisfactory interpretation. (At the back of this book, immediately following the poems, is a key indicating the biblical chapters and verses to which each poem corresponds.)

All translations are, by necessity, interpretations. My interpretations were based on linguistic investigations and, again, literary analysis — a process that took the form of an extended personal journey toward and away from the internal textures and contours of the text, as I tried to make the seemingly exotic metaphors of a distant culture come alive in a familar idiom. I was of course aware from the outset of the great impact that the King James Version has had on the ears of English readers. Rather than try to echo its rhythms or diction, I set out to create a fresh version that would open the locked gardens of the Hebrew. My aim was to probe the roots of the original and uncover resonances lost in other translations, but *not* to "Hebraize" English or mimic the aesthetic techniques of Hebrew verse. Rather than writing "translationese," I tried to write the best poetry I could.

After I finished work on the translation, the last step remaining to present the Song in English was to find a way to represent the three different kinds of voices that are grammatically distinguishable in the Hebrew — that is, the voice of a man, the voice of a woman, and the voice of a group of speakers. These are usually discernible in the original because in Hebrew, various parts of speech, including the pronoun "you," have gender and number. So, for example, if a speaker says "I love you" in Hebrew, we know whether a man or a woman is being addressed; by assuming a heterosexual relationship — a valid assumption for the Song — we can also deduce the gender of the speaker. Without such grammatical clues, it would be nearly impossible to know who is speaking and to whom, especially because the voices do not conform to masculine and feminine stereotypes. But English, unlike Hebrew, does not provide such grammatical clues to gender; hence the need to find another way to make these identifications.

I decided to use three different type styles to distinguish among voices in the English. Thus, throughout the translation, passages spoken by a female voice are in roman (as in poem 1), passages spoken by a male voice are in *italic* (as in poem 4), and passages spoken by a group of voices or by unidentifiable speakers are in **bold** (as in poem 11). Because many of the poems are dialogues and a few are spoken by three different speakers, different type styles appear within individual poems. In any given poem, each type style represents a consistent speaker, but the type styles do not necessarily imply consistent speakers from poem to poem. (For example, the female speaker of the first stanza of poem 7 is the same as the speaker of that poem's third stanza, but not necessarily the same as the female speaker of poem 8.)

Once set in three type styles, the English version of the Song was complete and ready for reading aloud — that necessary act of giving voice to words that brings all poetry to life. My hope was that by presenting the English poems in this form alongside the reconstructed and fully vocalized Hebrew poems (complete with the Masoretic accent marks that act as musical notation for chanting the text), I would make the Song available bilingually for a variety of uses and

occasions — from wedding ceremonies to Passover seders —
and thus help to keep its long and vibrant oral history alive
in our culture and time.

A final note: there are no — there cannot be — truly literal
translations of literary works. Yet, although none of my
translations even strives to be literal, all are attempts to draw
close to the meanings, intentions, and spirit of the original.
My aim has been fidelity — not to isolated images, but to the
meanings of images in their original cultural contexts and to
the effects they might have had on their earliest audience.
Thus, at times, my renditions will seem to depart radically
from other, more literal versions.

For example, in chapter 1, verse 9, of the Hebrew (the
opening lines of my poem 4), a woman is compared to a
mare in Pharaoh's chariotry — a puzzling image, for in that
context only stallions, never mares, drew chariots. But the
Egyptians' enemies set mares loose in war to drive the pharaoh's stallions wild, and this is the crux of the metaphor.
The woman is not simply a beautiful creature; she is as al-
luring as "a mare among stallions." Seen this way, the image
is striking and perhaps even daunting: the beloved possesses
a captivating power over her admirer. Yet his response is not
to withdraw but to draw nearer; although the beloved is
beautiful just as she is, the speaker, wanting to share love, offers to adorn her with his own gifts.

The poems in this book are a gift back to their source and
an attempt to share in the tradition.

THE
SONG *of*
SONGS

שִׁיר הַשִּׁירִים אֲשֶׁר לִשְׁלֹמֹה:

The Song of Songs

יִשָּׁקֵ֙נִי֙ מִנְּשִׁיק֣וֹת פִּ֔יהוּ
כִּֽי־טוֹבִ֥ים דֹּדֶ֖יךָ מִיָּֽיִן:
לְרֵ֙יחַ֙ שְׁמָנֶ֣יךָ טוֹבִ֔ים
שֶׁ֖מֶן תּוּרַ֣ק שְׁמֶ֑ךָ
עַל־כֵּ֖ן עֲלָמ֥וֹת אֲהֵבֽוּךָ:

מָשְׁכֵ֖נִי אַחֲרֶ֣יךָ נָּר֑וּצָה
הֱבִיאַ֙נִי֙ הַמֶּ֙לֶךְ֙ חֲדָרָ֔יו
נָגִ֥ילָה וְנִשְׂמְחָה֙ בָּ֔ךְ
נַזְכִּ֥ירָה דֹדֶ֙יךָ֙ מִיַּ֔יִן
מֵישָׁרִ֖ים אֲהֵבֽוּךָ:

O for your kiss! For your love
More enticing than wine,
For your scent and sweet name —
For all this they love you.

Take me away to your room,
Like a king to his rooms —
We'll rejoice there with wine.
No wonder they love you!

שְׁחוֹרָה אֲנִי וְנָאוָה
בְּנוֹת יְרוּשָׁלָ͏ֵם
כְּאָהֳלֵי קֵדָר
כִּירִיעוֹת שְׁלֹמֹה׃

אַל־תִּרְאוּנִי שֶׁאֲנִי שְׁחַרְחֹרֶת
שֶׁשֱּׁזָפַתְנִי הַשָּׁמֶשׁ

בְּנֵי אִמִּי נִחֲרוּ־בִי
שָׂמֻנִי נֹטֵרָה אֶת־הַכְּרָמִים
כַּרְמִי שֶׁלִּי לֹא נָטָרְתִּי׃

2

Yes, I am black! and radiant —
O city women watching me —
As black as Kedar's goathair tents
Or Solomon's fine tapestries.

Will you disrobe me with your stares?
The eyes of many morning suns
Have pierced my skin, and now I shine
Black as the light before the dawn.

And I have faced the angry glare
Of others, even my mother's sons
Who sent me out to watch their vines
While I neglected all my own.

הַגִּידָה לִּי שֶׁאָהֲבָה נַפְשִׁי
אֵיכָה תִרְעֶה
אֵיכָה תַּרְבִּיץ בַּצָּהֳרָיִם
שַׁלָּמָה אֶהְיֶה כְּעֹטְיָה
עַל עֶדְרֵי חֲבֵרֶיךָ:

אִם־לֹא תֵדְעִי לָךְ
הַיָּפָה בַּנָּשִׁים
צְאִי־לָךְ בְּעִקְבֵי הַצֹּאן
וּרְעִי אֶת־גְּדִיֹּתַיִךְ
עַל מִשְׁכְּנוֹת הָרֹעִים:

Tell me, my love, where you feed your sheep
And where you rest in the afternoon,
For why should I go searching blindly
Among the flocks of your friends?

If you don't know, O lovely woman,
Follow the tracks that the sheep have made
And feed your own little goats and lambs
In the fields where the shepherds lie.

לְסֻסָתִי֙ בְּרִכְבֵ֣י פַרְעֹ֔ה
דִּמִּיתִ֖יךְ רַעְיָתִֽי׃

נָאו֤וּ לְחָיַ֙יִךְ֙ בַּתֹּרִ֔ים
צַוָּארֵ֖ךְ בַּחֲרוּזִֽים׃

תּוֹרֵ֤י זָהָב֙ נַעֲשֶׂה־לָּ֔ךְ
עִ֖ם נְקֻדּ֥וֹת הַכָּֽסֶף׃

Like a mare among stallions,
You lure, I am held

    your cheeks framed with braids
    your neck traced with shells

I'll adorn you with gold
And with silver bells

עַד־שֶׁהַמֶּ֫לֶךְ בִּמְסִבּוֹ
נִרְדִּי נָתַן רֵיחוֹ:

צְרוֹר הַמֹּר ׀ דּוֹדִי לִי
בֵּין שָׁדַי יָלִין:

אֶשְׁכֹּל הַכֹּ֫פֶר ׀ דּוֹדִי לִי
בְּכַרְמֵי עֵין גֶּ֫דִי:

5

Until the king returns
    I lie in fragrance,
Sweet anticipation
    Of his entrance.

Between my breasts he'll lie —
    Sachet of spices,
Spray of blossoms plucked
    From the oasis.

הִנָּךְ יָפָה רַעְיָתִי
הִנָּךְ יָפָה
עֵינַיִךְ יוֹנִים:

הִנְּךָ יָפֶה דוֹדִי
אַף נָעִים
אַף־עַרְשֵׂנוּ רַעֲנָנָה:
קֹרוֹת בָּתֵּינוּ אֲרָזִים
*רַחִיטֵנוּ בְּרוֹתִים:

*רַהִיטֵנוּ

How fine
you are, my love,
your eyes
like doves'.

How fine
are you, my lover,
what joy
we have together.

How green
our bed of leaves,
our rafters of cedars,
our juniper eaves.

אֲנִי חֲבַצֶּלֶת הַשָּׁרוֹן
שׁוֹשַׁנַּת הָעֲמָקִים:

כְּשׁוֹשַׁנָּה בֵּין הַחוֹחִים
כֵּן רַעְיָתִי בֵּין הַבָּנוֹת:

כְּתַפּוּחַ בַּעֲצֵי הַיַּעַר
כֵּן דּוֹדִי בֵּין הַבָּנִים
בְּצִלּוֹ חִמַּדְתִּי וְיָשַׁבְתִּי
וּפִרְיוֹ מָתוֹק לְחִכִּי:

7

In sandy earth or deep
In valley soil
I grow, a wildflower thriving
On your love.

Narcissus in the brambles,
Brightest flower—
I choose you from all others
For my love.

Sweet fruit tree growing wild
Within the thickets—
I blossom in your shade
And taste your love.

ח

הֱבִיאַנִי אֶל־בֵּית הַיַּיִן
וְדִגְלוֹ עָלַי אַהֲבָה:

סַמְּכוּנִי בָּאֲשִׁישׁוֹת
רַפְּדוּנִי בַּתַּפּוּחִים
כִּי־חוֹלַת אַהֲבָה אָנִי:

שְׂמֹאלוֹ תַּחַת לְרֹאשִׁי
וִימִינוֹ תְּחַבְּקֵנִי:

הִשְׁבַּעְתִּי אֶתְכֶם בְּנוֹת יְרוּשָׁלַם
בִּצְבָאוֹת אוֹ בְּאַיְלוֹת הַשָּׂדֶה
אִם־תָּעִירוּ ׀ וְאִם־תְּעוֹרְרוּ
אֶת־הָאַהֲבָה עַד שֶׁתֶּחְפָּץ:

8

He brings me to the winehall,
Gazing at me with love.

Feed me raisincakes and quinces!
For I am sick with love.

O for his arms around me,
Beneath me and above!

O women of the city,
Swear by the wild field doe

Not to wake or rouse us
Till we fulfill our love.

קוֹל דּוֹדִי הִנֵּה־זֶה בָּא
מְדַלֵּג עַל־הֶהָרִים
מְקַפֵּץ עַל־הַגְּבָעוֹת:
דּוֹמֶה דוֹדִי לִצְבִי
אוֹ לְעֹפֶר הָאַיָּלִים
הִנֵּה־זֶה עוֹמֵד אַחַר כָּתְלֵנוּ
מַשְׁגִּיחַ מִן־הַחַלֹּנוֹת
מֵצִיץ מִן־הַחֲרַכִּים:

עָנָה דוֹדִי וְאָמַר לִי

קוּמִי לָךְ רַעְיָתִי
יָפָתִי וּלְכִי־לָךְ:

כִּי־הִנֵּה *הַסְּתָו עָבָר   *הַסְּתָיו
הַגֶּשֶׁם חָלַף הָלַךְ לוֹ:
הַנִּצָּנִים נִרְאוּ בָאָרֶץ
עֵת הַזָּמִיר הִגִּיעַ
וְקוֹל הַתּוֹר נִשְׁמַע בְּאַרְצֵנוּ:
הַתְּאֵנָה חָנְטָה פַגֶּיהָ
וְהַגְּפָנִים ׀ סְמָדַר נָתְנוּ רֵיחַ

קוּמִי *לָכִי רַעְיָתִי   *לָךְ
יָפָתִי וּלְכִי־לָךְ:

9

The sound of my lover
coming from the hills
quickly, like a deer
upon the mountains

Now at my windows,
walking by the walls,
here at the lattices
he calls —

Come with me,
my love,
come away

For the long wet months are past,
the rains have fed the earth
and left it bright with blossoms

Birds wing in the low sky,
dove and songbird singing
in the open air above

Earth nourishing tree and vine,
green fig and tender grape,
green and tender fragrance

Come with me,
my love,
come away

יוֹנָתִי בְּחַגְוֵי הַסֶּלַע
בְּסֵתֶר הַמַּדְרֵגָה
הַרְאִינִי אֶת־מַרְאַיִךְ
הַשְׁמִיעִנִי אֶת־קוֹלֵךְ
כִּי־קוֹלֵךְ עָרֵב
וּמַרְאֵיךְ נָאוֶה:

My dove
    in the clefts
        of the rocks
    the secret
        of steep ravines

Come let me look at you
Come let me hear you

    Your voice clear as water
    Your beautiful body

Like a mare among stallions,
You lure, I am held

My dove
in the clefts
of the rocks

אֶחֱזוּ־לָנוּ שׁוּעָלִים
שׁוּעָלִים קְטַנִּים
מְחַבְּלִים כְּרָמִים
וּכְרָמֵינוּ סְמָדָר:

II

Catch the foxes!
    the little foxes
    among the vines
Catch the foxes!
    the quick little foxes
    raiding the new grapes
    on our vines

דּוֹדִי לִי וַאֲנִי לוֹ
הָרֹעֶה בַּשׁוֹשַׁנִּים:

עַד שֶׁיָּפוּחַ הַיּוֹם
וְנָסוּ הַצְּלָלִים
סֹב דְּמֵה-לְךָ
דוֹדִי לִצְבִי
אוֹ לְעֹפֶר הָאַיָּלִים
עַל-הָרֵי בָתֶר:

12

My lover turns to me,
I turn to him,
Who leads his flock to feed
Among the flowers.

Until the day is over
And the shadows flee,
Turn round, my lover,
Go quickly, and be
Like deer or gazelles
In the clefts of the hills.

עַל־מִשְׁכָּבִי בַּלֵּילוֹת
בִּקַּשְׁתִּי אֵת שֶׁאָהֲבָה נַפְשִׁי
בִּקַּשְׁתִּיו וְלֹא מְצָאתִיו:

אָקוּמָה נָּא וַאֲסוֹבְבָה בָעִיר
בַּשְּׁוָקִים וּבָרְחֹבוֹת
אֲבַקְשָׁה אֵת שֶׁאָהֲבָה נַפְשִׁי
בִּקַּשְׁתִּיו וְלֹא מְצָאתִיו:

מְצָאוּנִי הַשֹּׁמְרִים הַסֹּבְבִים בָּעִיר
אֵת שֶׁאָהֲבָה נַפְשִׁי רְאִיתֶם:
כִּמְעַט שֶׁעָבַרְתִּי מֵהֶם
עַד שֶׁמָּצָאתִי אֵת שֶׁאָהֲבָה נַפְשִׁי

אֲחַזְתִּיו וְלֹא אַרְפֶּנּוּ
עַד־שֶׁהֲבֵיאתִיו אֶל־בֵּית אִמִּי
וְאֶל־חֶדֶר הוֹרָתִי:

הִשְׁבַּעְתִּי אֶתְכֶם בְּנוֹת יְרוּשָׁלַם
בִּצְבָאוֹת אוֹ בְּאַיְלוֹת הַשָּׂדֶה
אִם־תָּעִירוּ וְאִם־תְּעוֹרְרוּ
אֶת־הָאַהֲבָה עַד שֶׁתֶּחְפָּץ:

13

At night in bed, I want him—
The one I love is not here.

I'll rise and search the city,
Through the streets and squares

Until the city watchmen
Find me wandering there

And I ask them—have you seen him?
The one I love is not here.

When they have gone, I find him
And I won't let him go

Until he's in my mother's home,
The room where I was born.

O women of the city,
Swear by the wild field doe

Not to wake or rouse us
Till we fulfill our love.

מִי זֹאת עֹלָה֙ מִן־הַמִּדְבָּ֔ר
כְּתִֽימְרֹ֖ות עָשָׁ֑ן
מְקֻטֶּ֤רֶת מֹור֙ וּלְבֹונָ֔ה
מִכֹּ֖ל אַבְקַ֥ת רֹוכֵֽל׃

הִנֵּ֗ה מִטָּתֹו֙ שֶׁלִּשְׁלֹמֹ֔ה
שִׁשִּׁ֥ים גִּבֹּרִ֖ים סָבִ֣יב לָ֑הּ
מִגִּבֹּרֵ֖י יִשְׂרָאֵֽל׃
כֻּלָּם֙ אֲחֻ֣זֵי חֶ֔רֶב
מְלֻמְּדֵ֖י מִלְחָמָ֑ה
אִ֤ישׁ חַרְבֹּו֙ עַל־יְרֵכֹ֔ו
מִפַּ֖חַד בַּלֵּילֹֽות׃

אַפִּרְיֹ֗ון עָ֤שָׂה לֹו֙
הַמֶּ֣לֶךְ שְׁלֹמֹ֔ה
מֵעֲצֵ֖י הַלְּבָנֹֽון׃
עַמּוּדָיו֙ עָ֣שָׂה כֶ֔סֶף
רְפִידָתֹ֣ו זָהָ֔ב
מֶרְכָּבֹ֖ו אַרְגָּמָ֑ן
תֹּוכֹו֙ רָצ֣וּף אַהֲבָ֔ה
מִבְּנֹ֖ות יְרוּשָׁלָֽ͏ִם׃

צְאֶ֧ינָה ׀ וּֽרְאֶ֛ינָה בְּנֹ֥ות צִיֹּ֖ון
בַּמֶּ֣לֶךְ שְׁלֹמֹ֑ה
בָּעֲטָרָ֗ה שֶׁעִטְּרָה־לֹּ֤ו אִמֹּו֙
בְּיֹ֣ום חֲתֻנָּתֹ֔ו
וּבְיֹ֖ום שִׂמְחַ֥ת לִבֹּֽו׃

14

Who is this approaching, up from the desert
In columns of smoke, fragrant with incense,
Rare spices and herbs of the wandering merchants?

Behold, it appears—the king's own procession
Attended by sixty of Israel's warriors,
Swords at their thighs to meet the night's dangers.

A carriage of cedar with pillars of silver,
Gold floor, purple cushions, all made to his orders
And fashioned with love by Jerusalem's daughters.

Go out and see, O Jerusalem's daughters!
Crowned by his mother, the king in his carriage
This day of rejoicing, this day of his marriage.

הִנָּךְ יָפָה רַעְיָתִי
הִנָּךְ יָפָה
עֵינַיִךְ יוֹנִים
מִבַּעַד לְצַמָּתֵךְ

שַׂעְרֵךְ כְּעֵדֶר הָעִזִּים
שֶׁגָּלְשׁוּ מֵהַר גִּלְעָד:

שִׁנַּיִךְ כְּעֵדֶר הַקְּצוּבוֹת
שֶׁעָלוּ מִן־הָרַחְצָה
שֶׁכֻּלָּם מַתְאִימוֹת
וְשַׁכֻּלָה אֵין בָּהֶם:

כְּחוּט הַשָּׁנִי שִׂפְתֹתַיִךְ
וּמִדְבָּרֵךְ נָאוֶה

כְּפֶלַח הָרִמּוֹן רַקָּתֵךְ
מִבַּעַד לְצַמָּתֵךְ:

כְּמִגְדַּל דָּוִיד צַוָּארֵךְ
בָּנוּי לְתַלְפִּיּוֹת
אֶלֶף הַמָּגֵן תָּלוּי עָלָיו
כֹּל שִׁלְטֵי הַגִּבּוֹרִים:

שְׁנֵי שָׁדַיִךְ כִּשְׁנֵי עֳפָרִים
תְּאוֹמֵי צְבִיָּה
הָרוֹעִים בַּשּׁוֹשַׁנִּים:

15

How fine
you are, my love,
your eyes like doves'
behind your veil

Your hair—
as black as goats
winding down the slopes

Your teeth—
a flock of sheep
rising from the stream
in twos, each with its twin

Your lips—
like woven threads
of crimson silk

A gleam of pomegranate—
your forehead
through your veil

Your neck—
a tower
adorned with shields

Your breasts—
twin fawns
in fields of flowers

עַד שֶׁיָּפֹוּחַ הַיּוֹם
וְנָסוּ הַצְּלָלִים
אֵלֶךְ לִי אֶל־הַר הַמּוֹר
וְאֶל־גִּבְעַת הַלְּבוֹנָה:

כֻּלָּךְ יָפָה רַעְיָתִי
וּמוּם אֵין בָּךְ:

Until
the day is over,
shadows gone,

I'll go
up to the hills
of fragrant bloom

How fine
you are, my love,
my perfect one

טז

אִתִּי מִלְּבָנוֹן כַּלָּה
אִתִּי מִלְּבָנוֹן תָּבוֹאִי
תָּשׁוּרִי ׀ מֵרֹאשׁ אֲמָנָה
מֵרֹאשׁ שְׂנִיר וְחֶרְמוֹן
מִמְּעֹנוֹת אֲרָיוֹת
מֵהַרְרֵי נְמֵרִים:

16

With me, my bride of the mountains,
Come away with me, come away!

Come down from the peaks of the mountains,
From the perilous Lebanon caves,

From the lairs where lions crouch hidden,
Where leopards watch nightly for prey,

Look down, look down and come away!

לִבַּבְתִּנִי אֲחֹתִי כַלָּה

לִבַּבְתִּנִי *בְּאַחַד מֵעֵינַיִךְ

בְּאַחַד עֲנָק מִצַּוְּרֹנָיִךְ:

*בְּאַחַת

מַה־יָּפוּ דֹדַיִךְ אֲחֹתִי כַלָּה

מַה־טֹּבוּ דֹדַיִךְ מִיַּיִן

וְרֵיחַ שְׁמָנַיִךְ מִכָּל־בְּשָׂמִים:

נֹפֶת תִּטֹּפְנָה שִׂפְתוֹתַיִךְ כַּלָּה

דְּבַשׁ וְחָלָב תַּחַת לְשׁוֹנֵךְ

וְרֵיחַ שַׂלְמֹתַיִךְ כְּרֵיחַ לְבָנוֹן:

17

With one flash of your eyes, you excite me,
One jewel on your neck stirs my heart,
    O my sister, my bride.

Your love, more than wine, is enticing,
Your fragrance is finer than spices,
    My sister, my bride.

Your lips, sweet with nectar, invite me
To honey and milk on your tongue,
    O my sister, my bride.

And even your clothing is fragrant
As wind from the Lebanon mountains,
    My sister, my bride.

גַּן ׀ נָעוּל אֲחֹתִי כַלָּה
גַּל נָעוּל מַעְיָן חָתוּם:
שְׁלָחַיִךְ פַּרְדֵּס רִמּוֹנִים
עִם פְּרִי מְגָדִים
כְּפָרִים עִם־נְרָדִים:
נֵרְדְּ ׀ וְכַרְכֹּם קָנֶה וְקִנָּמוֹן
עִם כָּל־עֲצֵי לְבוֹנָה
מֹר וַאֲהָלוֹת
עִם כָּל־רָאשֵׁי בְשָׂמִים:
מַעְיַן גַּנִּים
בְּאֵר מַיִם חַיִּים
וְנֹזְלִים מִן־לְבָנוֹן:

עוּרִי צָפוֹן וּבוֹאִי תֵימָן
הָפִיחִי גַנִּי יִזְּלוּ בְשָׂמָיו
יָבֹא דוֹדִי לְגַנּוֹ
וְיֹאכַל פְּרִי מְגָדָיו:

בָּאתִי לְגַנִּי אֲחֹתִי כַלָּה
אָרִיתִי מוֹרִי עִם־בְּשָׂמִי
אָכַלְתִּי יַעְרִי עִם־דִּבְשִׁי
שָׁתִיתִי יֵינִי עִם־חֲלָבִי

אִכְלוּ רֵעִים
שְׁתוּ וְשִׁכְרוּ דּוֹדִים:

18

Enclosed and hidden, you are a garden,
A still pool, a fountain.

Stretching your limbs, you open—
A field of pomegranates blooms,

Treasured fruit among the blossoms,
Henna, sweet cane, bark, and saffron,

Fragrant woods and succulents,
The finest spices and perfumes.

Living water, you are a fountain,
A well, a river flowing from the mountains.

Come, north winds and south winds!
Breathe upon my garden,

Bear its fragrance to my lover,
Let him come and share its treasures.

My bride, my sister, I have come
To gather spices in my garden,

To taste wild honey with my wine,
Milk and honey with my wine.

Feast, drink—and drink deeply—lovers!

יט

אֲנִי יְשֵׁנָה וְלִבִּי עֵר
קוֹל ׀ דּוֹדִי דוֹפֵק

פִּתְחִי־לִי אֲחֹתִי רַעְיָתִי
יוֹנָתִי תַמָּתִי
שֶׁרֹאשִׁי נִמְלָא־טָל
קְוֻּצּוֹתַי רְסִיסֵי לָיְלָה:

פָּשַׁטְתִּי אֶת־כֻּתָּנְתִּי
אֵיכָכָה אֶלְבָּשֶׁנָּה
רָחַצְתִּי אֶת־רַגְלַי
אֵיכָכָה אֲטַנְּפֵם:

דּוֹדִי שָׁלַח יָדוֹ מִן־הַחֹר
וּמֵעַי הָמוּ עָלָיו:

קַמְתִּי אֲנִי לִפְתֹּחַ לְדוֹדִי
וְיָדַי נָטְפוּ־מוֹר
וְאֶצְבְּעֹתַי מוֹר עֹבֵר
עַל כַּפּוֹת הַמַּנְעוּל:

פָּתַחְתִּי אֲנִי לְדוֹדִי
וְדוֹדִי חָמַק עָבָר
נַפְשִׁי יָצְאָה בְדַבְּרוֹ
בִּקַּשְׁתִּיהוּ וְלֹא מְצָאתִיהוּ
קְרָאתִיו וְלֹא עָנָנִי:

מְצָאֻנִי הַשֹּׁמְרִים הַסֹּבְבִים בָּעִיר
הִכּוּנִי פְצָעוּנִי
נָשְׂאוּ אֶת־רְדִידִי מֵעָלַי
שֹׁמְרֵי הַחֹמוֹת:

19

I sleep, but my heart stirs,
restless,
      and dreams . . .

My lover's voice here, at the door —

Open, my love, my sister,
my dove, my perfect one,
for my hair is soaked with the night.

Should I get up, get dressed,
and dirty my feet?

My love thrusts his hand at the latch
and my heart leaps for him!

I rise to open for my love,
my hands dripping perfume on the lock —

I open,
but he has gone.

I run out after him, calling,
but he is gone.

The men who roam the streets,
guarding the walls,
beat me and tear away my robe.

הִשְׁבַּעְתִּי אֶתְכֶם בְּנוֹת יְרוּשָׁלָ͏ִם
אִם־תִּמְצְאוּ אֶת־דּוֹדִי
מַה־תַּגִּידוּ לוֹ
שֶׁחוֹלַת אַהֲבָה אָנִי:

מַה־דּוֹדֵךְ מִדּוֹד
הַיָּפָה בַּנָּשִׁים
מַה־דּוֹדֵךְ מִדּוֹד
שֶׁכָּכָה הִשְׁבַּעְתָּנוּ:

דּוֹדִי צַח וְאָדוֹם
דָּגוּל מֵרְבָבָה:

רֹאשׁוֹ כֶּתֶם פָּז
קְוֻצּוֹתָיו תַּלְתַּלִּים
שְׁחֹרוֹת כָּעוֹרֵב:

עֵינָיו כְּיוֹנִים
עַל־אֲפִיקֵי מָיִם
רֹחֲצוֹת בֶּחָלָב
יֹשְׁבוֹת עַל־מִלֵּאת:

לְחָיָו כַּעֲרוּגַת הַבֹּשֶׂם
מִגְדְּלוֹת מֶרְקָחִים
שִׂפְתוֹתָיו שׁוֹשַׁנִּים
נֹטְפוֹת מוֹר עֹבֵר:

יָדָיו גְּלִילֵי זָהָב
מְמֻלָּאִים בַּתַּרְשִׁישׁ
מֵעָיו עֶשֶׁת שֵׁן
מְעֻלֶּפֶת סַפִּירִים:

O women of the city,
Swear to me!
If you find my lover
You will say
That I am sick with love.

**Who is your love
And why do you bind us by oath?**

My love is radiant
As gold or crimson,
Hair in waves of black
Like wings of ravens.

Eyes like doves, afloat
Upon the water,
Bathed in milk, at rest
On brimming pools.

Cheeks like beds of spices,
Banks of flowers,
Lips like lilies, sweet
And wet with dew.

Studded with jewels, his arms
Are round and golden,
His belly smooth as ivory,
Bright with gems.

שׁוֹקָיו֙ עַמּוּדֵי שֵׁשׁ
מְיֻסָּדִים עַל־אַדְנֵי־פָז

מַרְאֵ֙הוּ֙ כַּלְּבָנ֔וֹן
בָּח֖וּר כָּאֲרָזִים:

חִכּוֹ֙ מַֽמְתַקִּים
וְכֻלּ֖וֹ מַחֲמַדִּים

זֶ֤ה דוֹדִי֙ וְזֶ֣ה רֵעִ֔י
בְּנ֖וֹת יְרוּשָׁלָ֑ם:

אָ֚נָה הָלַ֣ךְ דּוֹדֵ֔ךְ
הַיָּפָ֖ה בַּנָּשִׁ֑ים
אָ֚נָה פָּנָ֣ה דוֹדֵ֔ךְ
וּנְבַקְשֶׁ֖נּוּ עִמָּֽךְ:

דּוֹדִי֙ יָרַ֣ד לְגַנּ֔וֹ
לַעֲרוּג֖וֹת הַבֹּ֑שֶׂם
לִרְעוֹת֙ בַּגַּנִּ֔ים
וְלִלְקֹ֖ט שֽׁוֹשַׁנִּֽים:

אֲנִ֤י לְדוֹדִי֙ וְדוֹדִ֣י לִ֔י
הָרֹעֶ֖ה בַּשּֽׁוֹשַׁנִּֽים:

Set in gold, his legs,
Two marble columns —
He stands as proud as cedars
In the mountains.

Man of pleasure — sweet
To taste his love!
Friend and lover chosen
For my love.

*B*eautiful woman,
*W*here has your lover gone to?
*W*here has he gone?
*W*e'll help you look for him.

My love has gone to walk
Within his garden —
To feed his sheep and there
To gather flowers.

I turn to meet my love,
He'll turn to me,
Who leads his flock to feed
Among the flowers.

From the lairs where lions crouch hidden,
Where leopards watch nightly for prey

Hair in waves of black
Like wings of ravens

יָפָה אַתְּ רַעְיָתִי כְּתִרְצָה
נָאוָה כִּירוּשָׁלָ͏ִם
אֲיֻמָּה כַּנִּדְגָּלוֹת:
הָסֵבִּי עֵינַיִךְ מִנֶּגְדִּי
שֶׁהֵם הִרְהִיבֻנִי

שַׂעְרֵךְ כְּעֵדֶר הָעִזִּים
שֶׁגָּלְשׁוּ מִן־הַגִּלְעָד:
שִׁנַּיִךְ כְּעֵדֶר הָרְחֵלִים
שֶׁעָלוּ מִן־הָרַחְצָה
שֶׁכֻּלָּם מַתְאִימוֹת
וְשַׁכֻּלָה אֵין בָּהֶם:
כְּפֶלַח הָרִמּוֹן רַקָּתֵךְ
מִבַּעַד לְצַמָּתֵךְ:

שִׁשִּׁים הֵמָּה מְלָכוֹת
וּשְׁמֹנִים פִּילַגְשִׁים
וַעֲלָמוֹת אֵין מִסְפָּר:
אַחַת הִיא יוֹנָתִי תַמָּתִי
אַחַת הִיא לְאִמָּהּ
בָּרָה הִיא לְיוֹלַדְתָּהּ
רָאוּהָ בָנוֹת וַיְאַשְּׁרוּהָ
מְלָכוֹת וּפִילַגְשִׁים וַיְהַלְלוּהָ:

מִי־זֹאת הַנִּשְׁקָפָה כְּמוֹ־שָׁחַר
יָפָה כַלְּבָנָה
בָּרָה כַּחַמָּה
אֲיֻמָּה כַּנִּדְגָּלוֹת:

20

Striking as Tirza
    you are, my love,
Bright as Jerusalem,
    frightening as visions!
Lower your eyes
    for they make me tremble

Your hair—as black as goats
    winding down the slopes
Your teeth—a flock of sheep
    rising from the stream
    in twos, each with its twin
A gleam of pomegranate—
    your forehead through your veil

Sixty queens, eighty brides,
    endless numbers of women—
One is my dove, my perfect one,
    pure as an only child—
Women see her
    and sing of her joy,
Queens and brides
    chant her praise

Who is she? staring
    down like the dawn's eye,
Bright as the white moon,
    pure as the hot sun,
Frightening as visions!

אֶל־גִּנַּת אֱגוֹז יָרַ֫דְתִּי
לִרְאוֹת בְּאִבֵּי הַנָּ֫חַל
לִרְאוֹת הֲפָרְחָה הַגֶּ֫פֶן
הֵנֵ֫צוּ הָרִמֹּנִים:

לֹא יָדַ֫עְתִּי נַפְשִׁי שָׂמַ֫תְנִי מַרְכְּבוֹת עַמִּי־נָדִיב:

21

Walking through the walnut orchard,
Looking for the signs of spring:
The pomegranates — have they flowered?
The grapevines — are they blossoming?

שׁוּבִי שׁוּבִי֙ הַשּׁוּלַמִּ֔ית
שׁוּבִי שׁ֖וּבִי וְנֶחֱזֶה־בָּ֑ךְ

מַה־תֶּחֱזוּ֙ בַּשּׁ֣וּלַמִּ֔ית
כִּמְחֹלַ֖ת הַֽמַּחֲנָֽיִם׃

מַה־יָּפ֧וּ פְעָמַ֛יִךְ
בַּנְּעָלִ֖ים בַּת־נָדִ֑יב
חַמּוּקֵ֣י יְרֵכַ֔יִךְ כְּמ֣וֹ חֲלָאִ֔ים
מַעֲשֵׂ֖ה יְדֵ֥י אָמָּֽן׃

שָׁרְרֵךְ֙ אַגַּ֣ן הַסַּ֔הַר
אַל־יֶחְסַ֖ר הַמָּ֑זֶג
בִּטְנֵךְ֙ עֲרֵמַ֣ת חִטִּ֔ים
סוּגָ֖ה בַּשּׁוֹשַׁנִּֽים׃

שְׁנֵ֥י שָׁדַ֛יִךְ כִּשְׁנֵ֥י עֳפָרִ֖ים
תָּאֳמֵ֥י צְבִיָּֽה׃

צַוָּארֵ֖ךְ כְּמִגְדַּ֣ל הַשֵּׁ֑ן
עֵינַ֜יִךְ בְּרֵכ֣וֹת בְּחֶשְׁבּ֗וֹן
עַל־שַׁ֙עַר֙ בַּת־רַבִּ֔ים
אַפֵּךְ֙ כְּמִגְדַּ֣ל הַלְּבָנ֔וֹן
צוֹפֶ֖ה פְּנֵ֥י דַמָּֽשֶׂק׃

רֹאשֵׁ֤ךְ עָלַ֙יִךְ֙ כַּכַּרְמֶ֔ל
וְדַלַּ֥ת רֹאשֵׁ֖ךְ כָּאַרְגָּמָ֑ן
מֶ֖לֶךְ אָס֥וּר בָּרְהָטִֽים׃

22

Dance for us, princess, dance,
  as we watch and chant!

What will you see as I move
  in the dance of love?

Your graceful, sandalled feet,
Your thighs—two spinning jewels,
Your hips—a bowl of nectar
  brimming full

Your belly—golden wheat
Adorned with daffodils,
Your breasts—two fawns, the twins
  of a gazelle

Your neck—an ivory tower,
Your eyes—two silent pools,
Your face—a tower that overlooks
  the hills

Your head—majestic mountain
Crowned with purple hair,
Captivating kings
  within its locks

מַה־יָּפִית וּמַה־נָּעַמְתְּ
אַהֲבָה בַּתַּעֲנוּגִים:

זֹאת קוֹמָתֵךְ דָּמְתָה לְתָמָר
וְשָׁדַיִךְ לְאַשְׁכֹּלוֹת:

אָמַרְתִּי אֶעֱלֶה בְתָמָר
אֹחֲזָה בְּסַנְסִנָּיו

וְיִהְיוּ־נָא שָׁדַיִךְ כְּאֶשְׁכְּלוֹת הַגֶּפֶן
וְרֵיחַ אַפֵּךְ כַּתַּפּוּחִים:

וְחִכֵּךְ כְּיֵין הַטּוֹב
הוֹלֵךְ לְדוֹדִי לְמֵישָׁרִים
דּוֹבֵב שִׂפְתֵי יְשֵׁנִים:

23

Of all pleasure, how sweet
Is the taste of love!

There you stand like a palm,
Your breasts clusters of dates.

Shall I climb that palm
And take hold of the boughs?

Your breasts will be tender
As clusters of grapes,

Your breath will be sweet
As the fragrance of quince,

And your mouth will awaken
All sleeping desire

Like wine that entices
The lips of new lovers.

אֲנִי לְדוֹדִי וְעָלַי תְּשׁוּקָתוֹ:

לְכָה דוֹדִי נֵצֵא הַשָּׂדֶה
נָלִינָה בַּכְּפָרִים:
נַשְׁכִּימָה לַכְּרָמִים
נִרְאֶה אִם פָּרְחָה הַגֶּפֶן
פִּתַּח הַסְּמָדַר
הֵנֵצוּ הָרִמּוֹנִים

שָׁם אֶתֵּן אֶת־דֹּדַי לָךְ:
הַדּוּדָאִים נָתְנוּ־רֵיחַ
וְעַל־פְּתָחֵינוּ כָּל־מְגָדִים
חֲדָשִׁים גַּם־יְשָׁנִים
דּוֹדִי צָפַנְתִּי לָךְ:

24

Turning to him, who meets me with desire —

Come, love, let us go out to the open fields
And spend our night lying where the henna blooms,
Rising early to leave for the near vineyards
Where the vines flower, opening tender buds,
And the pomegranate boughs unfold their blossoms.

There among blossom and vine I will give you my love,
Musk of the violet mandrakes spilled upon us . . .
And returning, finding our doorways piled with fruits,
The best of the new-picked and the long-stored,
My love, I will give you all I have saved for you.

Shall I climb that palm
And take hold of the boughs?

And the pomegranate boughs
  unfold their blossoms

מִי יִתֶּנְךָ כְּאָח לִי
יוֹנֵק שְׁדֵי אִמִּי
אֶמְצָאֲךָ בַחוּץ אֶשָּׁקְךָ
גַּם לֹא־יָבוּזוּ לִי:
אֶנְהָגְךָ אֲבִיאֲךָ
אֶל־בֵּית אִמִּי
תְּלַמְּדֵנִי
אַשְׁקְךָ מִיַּיִן הָרֶקַח
מֵעֲסִיס רִמֹּנִי:

שְׂמֹאלוֹ תַּחַת רֹאשִׁי
וִימִינוֹ תְּחַבְּקֵנִי:

הִשְׁבַּעְתִּי אֶתְכֶם בְּנוֹת יְרוּשָׁלָ͏ִם
מַה־תָּעִירוּ ׀ וּמַה־תְּעֹרְרוּ
אֶת־הָאַהֲבָה עַד שֶׁתֶּחְפָּץ:

25

Oh, if you were my brother
Nursed at my mother's breast,

I'd kiss you in the streets
And never suffer scorn.

I'd bring you to my mother's home
(My mother teaches me)

And give you wine and nectar
From my pomegranates.

O for his arms around me,
Beneath me and above!

O women of the city,
Swear by the wild field doe

Not to wake or rouse us
Till we fulfill our love.

מִי זֹאת עֹלָה֙ מִן־הַמִּדְבָּ֔ר
מִתְרַפֶּ֖קֶת עַל־דּוֹדָ֑הּ

*W*ho is this approaching,
   up from the wilderness,
      arm on her lover's arm?

תַּחַת הַתַּפּוּחַ עוֹרַרְתִּיךָ
שָׁמָּה חִבְּלַתְךָ אִמֶּךָ
שָׁמָּה חִבְּלָה יְלָדַתְךָ:

Under the quince tree
        you woke
        to my touch
there
        where she conceived
        where she who carried
        and bore you
conceived

שִׂימֵנִי כַחוֹתָם עַל־לִבֶּךָ
כַּחוֹתָם עַל־זְרוֹעֶךָ

כִּי־עַזָּה כַמָּוֶת אַהֲבָה
קָשָׁה כִשְׁאוֹל קִנְאָה
רְשָׁפֶיהָ רִשְׁפֵּי אֵשׁ
שַׁלְהֶבֶתְיָה:

מַיִם רַבִּים לֹא יוּכְלוּ
לְכַבּוֹת אֶת־הָאַהֲבָה
וּנְהָרוֹת לֹא יִשְׁטְפוּהָ

אִם־יִתֵּן אִישׁ
אֶת־כָּל־הוֹן בֵּיתוֹ בָּאַהֲבָה
בּוֹז יָבוּזוּ לוֹ:

28

Stamp me in your heart,
Upon your limbs,
Sear my emblem deep
Into your skin.

For love is strong as death,
Harsh as the grave.
Its tongues are flames, a fierce
And holy blaze.

Endless seas and floods,
Torrents and rivers
Never put out love's
Infinite fires.

Those who think that wealth
Can buy them love
Only play the fool
And meet with scorn.

אָחוֹת לָנוּ קְטַנָּה
וְשָׁדַיִם אֵין לָהּ
מַה־נַּעֲשֶׂה לַאֲחֹתֵנוּ
בַּיּוֹם שֶׁיְּדֻבַּר־בָּהּ:

אִם־חוֹמָה הִיא
נִבְנֶה עָלֶיהָ טִירַת כָּסֶף
וְאִם־דֶּלֶת הִיא
נָצוּר עָלֶיהָ לוּחַ אָרֶז:

אֲנִי חוֹמָה
וְשָׁדַי כַּמִּגְדָּלוֹת
אָז הָיִיתִי בְעֵינָיו
כְּמוֹצְאֵת שָׁלוֹם:

29

We have a young sister
Whose breasts are but flowers.
What shall we do
When the time comes for suitors?

If she's a wall
We'll build turrets of silver,
But if she's a door
We will plank her with cedar.

I am a wall
And my breasts are towers!
So I have found peace
Here with my lover.

כֶּרֶם הָיָה לִשְׁלֹמֹה
בְּבַעַל הָמוֹן
נָתַן אֶת־הַכֶּרֶם לַנֹּטְרִים
אִישׁ יָבִא בְּפִרְיוֹ
אֶלֶף כָּסֶף:

כַּרְמִי שֶׁלִּי לְפָנָי
הָאֶלֶף לְךָ שְׁלֹמֹה
וּמָאתַיִם לְנֹטְרִים אֶת־פִּרְיוֹ:

30

The king has a vineyard
Whose fruit is worth silver.
I have a vineyard—
Its fruit is my own.

Have your wealth, Solomon!
Keep all your vineyards,
Whose yield you must share
With your watchmen and guards.

הַיּוֹשֶׁבֶת בַּגַּנִּים
חֲבֵרִים מַקְשִׁיבִים לְקוֹלֵךְ
הַשְׁמִיעִינִי:

בְּרַח ׀ דּוֹדִי
וּדְמֵה־לְךָ לִצְבִי
אוֹ לְעֹפֶר הָאַיָּלִים
עַל הָרֵי בְשָׂמִים:

Woman
of the gardens,
of the voice
friends listen for,
will you let me hear you?

Go —
go now, my love,
be quick
as a gazelle
on the fragrant hills!

Key to the Biblical Text

Poem number followed by biblical chapter and verse:
Title — 1:1, 1 — 1:2-4, 2 — 1:5-6, 3 — 1:7-8, 4 — 1:9-11, 5 —
1:12-14, 6 — 1:15-17, 7 — 2:1-3, 8 — 2:4-7, 9 — 2:8-13, 10 —
2:14, 11 — 2:15, 12 — 2:16-17, 13 — 3:1-5, 14 — 3:6-11, 15 —
4:1-7, 16 — 4:8, 17 — 4:9-11, 18 — 4:12-5:1, 19 — 5:2-6:3, 20 —
6:4-10, 21 — 6:11,* 22 — 7:1-6, 23 — 7:7-10, 24 — 7:11-14, 25 —
8:1-4, 26 — 8:5a, 27 — 8:5b, 28 — 8:6-7, 29 — 8:8-10, 30 — 8:11-
12, 31 — 8:13-14.

*6:12 of the Hebrew has not been translated because its meaning is not de-
cipherable, but it has been presented at the bottom of the page on which the
Hebrew poem 21 appears.

Masoretic corrections are found in the margins of the Hebrew poems 6, 9,
and 17.

About the Translator

Marcia Falk, a widely published poet and translator, received her B.A. in philosophy from Brandeis University and her Ph.D. in English and comparative literature from Stanford University. She has been both a Fulbright Scholar and a Post-doctoral Fellow at the Hebrew University of Jerusalem, and has taught Hebrew and English literature and Hebrew Bible at Stanford, at the State University of New York at Binghamton, and at the Claremont Colleges. She is the recipient of two residency fellowships to the MacDowell Colony and of the Gertrude Claytor Award of the Poetry Society of America. Currently she is an Affiliated Scholar at Stanford's Institute for Research on Women and Gender and at the Bain Research Group of the University of California at Berkeley.

Marcia Falk's other books include two poetry collections, *It is July in Virginia* and *This Year in Jerusalem*, and a volume of translations from the Yiddish, *With Teeth in the Earth: Selected Poems of Malka Heifetz Tussman* (Wayne State University Press, 1992). She is currently writing *The Book of Blessings: A Feminist-Jewish Reconstruction of Prayer* (forthcoming from Harper San Francisco, 1993).

About This Edition

The Song of Songs was set in Mergenthaler Centaur, Arrighi, and Bembo Medium by Wilsted & Taylor, Oakland, California. Centaur, which was modelled on Jenson's roman, was designed by Bruce Rogers in 1914 as a titling font for the Metropolitan Museum of New York. Arrighi was designed by Frederic Warde to accompany Centaur, and was first cut for hand composition in 1925. Bembo was first used in 1495 in a publication by Cardinal Bembo and was the forerunner of two centuries of standard European type.

The Hebrew text was set in Hadassah by Simcha Graphics, Brooklyn, New York. Hadassah was created by Henri Friedlander, who is considered the master of Hebrew calligraphy today. Begun in Germany in the early 1930s, the design for Hadassah was interrupted by World War II and completed in the early 1950s in Israel. One of the first modern Hebrew text faces, it combines twentieth-century principles of design with elements of ancient calligraphic styles.

Those interested in reading more about the content and structure of the Song of Songs may see the clothbound edition of Marcia Falk's translation, *The Song of Songs: A New Translation and Interpretation*, published by Harper San Francisco in 1990. Aimed at general readers and Bible scholars alike, the cloth edition contains a six-chapter "Translator's Study," which treats these matters in depth.